The

BOOK OF FEARS AND PHOBIAS

Written By
John Ficarra

Illustrated By
Paul Coker, Jr.

WARNER BOOKS

A Warner Communications Company

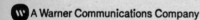

DEDICATED TO

Mary and Joe Honey,

The best parents a person
could ever hope for.

TABLE OF CONTENTS

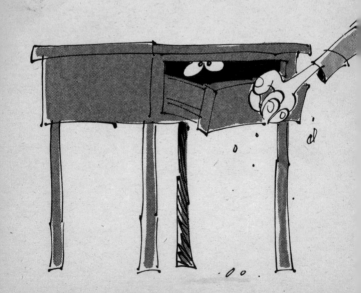

PART III

Fear is a basic, emotional response to a specific situation.

There are several forms of fear. There's **Anxiety;** a vague feeling in which a person fears what **may** happen.

There's also **Panic;** a sudden, unreasonable, overpowering fear.

And there's **Paranoia,** a fear in which a person believes he is being followed and watched.

Lastly, there is a **Phobia;** an intense fear of
something that others find small or
innocuous. Such as Ombrophobia;
the fear of rain.

Some fears may be inborn. For example, babies tend to be afraid of loud noises.

But as we get older we learn to recognize certain sounds . . .

. . . and we no longer fear them.

A fear may also be learned through a previous bad experience.

Often just a single word or simple phrase can provoke the most severe feeling of fear.

Upon hearing a strange noise, a deer tend
surrounding environment.

A cat frequently shows fe

first examine how animals show fear.

to freeze in its tracks and blend in with the

y making its hair stand up straight.

And a dog will show its fear by growling, barking loudly, and baring its teeth.

. . . Well, any self-respecting dog would!

Humans show fear in much the same way.

It is important to note that fear itself is not necessarily a bad thing. It can keep us from getting hurt,

. . . make us exercise more caution

. . . and even help us run faster than we
ever thought possible.

In some instances, you would be an absolute schmuck not to be fearful.

But of all the types of fear mentioned, it is generally agreed that the absolute worst of these, the one that can screw up your life the most, is the unnatural fear caused by the **phobia!**

What is a PHOBIA?

A phobia is an excessive, irrational and uncontrollable fear of a perfectly normal situation or object. Among the more common phobias are . . .

Claustrophobia (fear of enclosed spaces)

Musophobia (fear of mice)

Odontiatrophobia (fear of dentists),

and Hemophobia (fear of
the sight of blood).

Also . . .

Leprophobia (fear of leprosy).

and Geniophobia (fear of chins).

Among the less common phobias are . . .

Aerophobia (fear of breezes).

and Pediophobia (fear of ventriloquist's dummies).

The word phobia is from the Greek name "Phobos." Phobos was a minor Greek god who went with his war-god father into battle to spread fear among the enemy. This was history's first example of psychological warfare.

Most modern day terms for the various phobias are a result of the combining of the Greek word for that which is feared with the suffix "phobia." A good example of this is when we take the word "hydro" (which is Greek for "water") and add "phobia." Thus "Hydrophobia" is the fear of water.

A very stupid example of this same process can be seen when we take the word "phobia" (to fear) and add the suffix "phobia." This gives us . . .

. . . the fear of developing other fears.

Carrying this stupidity even further, it stands to reason that somewhere out in the world, some poor soul is suffering from . . .

. . . the fear of developing the fear of developing other fears. Confused? What do you want from us? We told you it was a stupid example!

Doctors estimate that as many as one out of every ten people in the English speaking world have some form of phobia.

Note: If you picked the man third from left, you are WRONG! The man third from the left has the flu and 102 temperature. The phobic is the man on the extreme right, Mr. Lats Calamia, who suffers from Stasiphobia, the fear of standing upright.

As for estimates of phobics in the non-English speaking world, doctors are less sure.

Phobias tend to appear gradually. Often so gradually that the person cannot remember how or when it all started. This sometimes makes treatment very difficult.

Complicating matters, some people **suffer** from Mnemophobia, the fear of memories. Every time they try to remember when it was they first became phobic, they become even more phobic!

Phobias fall into three basic categories:

The first category is the fear of a specific object, such as Xyrophobia . . .

. . . the fear of razors;

or Helminthophobia . . .

. . . the fear of worms.

In the second category, people fear a specific situation, such as Epistemophobia . . .

. . . the fear of being in school;

or Dikephobia . . .

. . . the fear of being in jail.

Lastly, there are the more abstract fears, such as Ideophobia . . .

. . . the fear of ideas;

and Taeniophobia . . .

. . . the fear of intestinal infestation.

In the first category — fear of a specific object — the cause of the phobia can often be traced to a single fright. For example, a person who suffers from Boustrophobia, the fear of cows, may at one time in his life have had a bad experience with a cow.

Or something closely associated with a cow.

Likewise, those phobias in the second category — fear of a specific situation — can usually be traced to a single, previous frightening experience. For example, while dining out one night, one man found a fly in his soup and now suffers from Phagophobia, the fear of restaurants.

. . . the "fly" he found in his soup
was the waiter's.

In the last category — abstract fears — a person may develop a phobia after being exposed to that which he now fears. For example, a person might develop Trichopathophobia, the fear of hair disease, after dating a person with a dandruff problem.

But regardless of how and why a phobia begins, once it starts, the miserable results are always the same. As you will see in our next section entitled . . .

DREADED PHOBIA SYMPTOMS

Once a phobic attack begins, a person can suffer numerous physiological symptoms. Among them . . .

. . . Sweating

. . . Butterflies in the stomach

. . . Hair standing on end

. . . Dilated pupils

. . . Trembling

. . . A dry, tight throat

. . . Dizziness

. . . Rapid heart pounding

. . . Nausea

... and finally an urge to run, scream and get the heck away from whatever is making him phobic.

Unfortunately, these symptoms are exactly the same ones that many people (especially teenagers and neurotic New Yorkers) experience when meeting and dating members of the opposite sex. This makes for a lousy puberty and a rather nasty situation in general.

So far in this book we have taken a look at the various kinds of fears and phobias, their causes and the symptoms they project. In Part II of this book, we will take an indepth look at some of the more common phobias, some current popular theories about them and what treatment is available to those afflicted.

A relatively new phobia which doctors are just now beginning to diagnose and examine is Technophobia — the fear of computers and other high-tech pieces of machinery.

It seems as if the computer has invaded every part of our daily lives. Thanks to the micro-chip, we now have computerized talking clocks . . .

. . . talking microwave ovens,

. . . and talking cars.

There are gizmos that . . . tape music when you're not home . . . record television shows while you're not home . . . start dinner when you're not home . . . and even answer the phone when you're not home.

All these innovations and inventions were supposed to make life easier and better for the average person.

. . . Once the average person has figured out how to work all this stuff, that is!

But a strange thing happened. Instead of embracing all these gadgets, many people hated them!

From the start, some people refused to have anything to do with them and hung on to their old ways of doing things.

Others bought some high-tech stuff, but stopped using it almost immediately.

And some people actually started to **FEAR** what the computer revolution had wrought. These people were the first victims of Technophobia!

Because it is so new, doctors are just now beginning to explore the many reasons behind Technophobia.

One conclusion doctors seem certain of is that many people fear computers because of the strange language computer programmers use when discussing these machines.

Doctors discovered that these words and phrases (commonly referred to as "computerese" or "technobabble") conjure-up all sorts of mysterious and weird mental pictures in the victim's mind, which in turn trigger . . .

. . . you guessed it, a phobic attack.

To demonstrate this phenomenon, a sampling of the most commonly used computer terms was gathered and read to a victim of Technophobia. The victim was then asked to describe what came into his mind when he heard these phrases.

The results of this little experiment follow in the next section of this book entitled . . .

"A HACKER gaining access"

"Moving a CURSOR"

"Swapping 32 BYTES"

"Upgrading a MEMORY"

"The graceful degradation of a PERIPHERAL"

"A BIT TWIDDLER Committing a GRAUNCH"

"Gang punching a BATCH"

"Eating a CRUFTY DISC"

"Running a PROGRAM"

"Calling up an OLD FILE"

"Uncovering a GLITCH"

"Debugging a MODEM"

"Executing a DUMMY ROUTINE"

If a person is afraid of all animals, then he is suffering from Zoophobia — even if the animals he fears the most aren't necessarily found in a zoo.

Some people fear only certain animals. For example, a person who suffers from Ornithophobia has a fear of birds.

A person who suffers from
Batrachophobia has a fear
of frogs.

And a person who is stricken with Ichthyophobia fears fish.

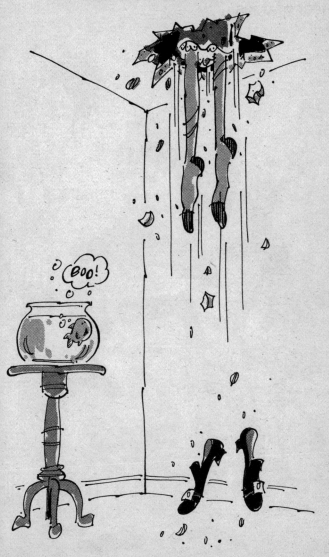

There frequently are off-shoots of animal phobias. For example, Cynophobia is the fear of dogs.

Cynosplatophobia is a fear of dogs that haven't been housebroken.

Likewise, the fear of bulls is known as Boustrophobia.

However, the fear of throwing the bull is known as Insurancesalesmanophobia.

Fear of insects is also very common. The fear of all insects in general is known as Entomophobia.

Fear of small insects only is known as Acarophobia.

The fear of stinging insects only is known as Melissophobia.

And the fear of just spiders is known as Arachneophobia .

The name of the phobia for the fear of all spiders, in general, but in particular, ones which are small and sting, takes three days to type and even longer to pronounce. It rarely comes up in conversation.

AGORAPHOBIA

(Fear of Public Places)

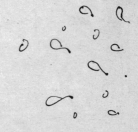

One of the worst phobias a person can suffer from is Agoraphobia — the fear of open or public places. Little is known about this crippling phobia which often results in the victim's fear of leaving home.

One strange fact doctors have uncovered is that two-thirds of Agoraphobic victims are female.

Let's rephrase that. Two out of every three Agoraphobia victims are female.

Doctors say that among the classic beginning symptoms of Agoraphobia are . . .

. . . nervous irritability,

. . . sleeplessness,

. . . and loss of appetite.

. . . All followed by a constant state of impending doom when away from home.

There are, however, other less classic signs that you may be Agoraphobic. For example:

If you insist that garbagemen pick up your garbage in your kitchen;

If you once had major surgery at home rather than go to a hospital...

... and if you have a special clause in your will that stipulates that you must be buried in your living room;

... chances are you are Agoraphobic.

Since Agoraphobia is so widespread (one in every 100 people) there are numerous therapy groups around the country. As you might suspect, low attendance at the meetings is often a big problem.

Nevertheless, doctors maintain that all phobias, including Agoraphobia, can be greatly controlled and even cured through a process known as Exposure Therapy, as we shall see in the next section of the book entitled . . .

THE TREATMENT OF

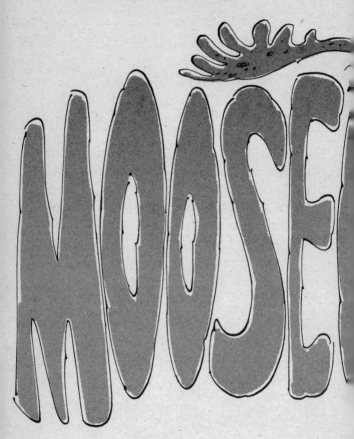

The most widespread and effective treatment of any phobia involves Exposure Therapy — the gradual exposure of the victim to that place or thing of which he is now phobic.

For example, let us see how a doctor might treat a patient who suffers from the fear of moose which, for our purposes, shall henceforth be known as Mooseophobia.

The first step a doctor might take is to write the word "moose" on a blackboard and perhaps add a simple sketch of a moose.

Next, the doctor might suggest that the patient begin carrying a picture of a moose

. . . Though not necessarily the same picture the doctor drew on the blackboard!

As the patient becomes more and more comfortable with the thought of a moose, the doctor might then prescribe a movie or TV show which features a moose.

Treatment would then enter the most important stage — the gradual introduction of the patient to a real, live moose. This must be accomplished slowly.

Very slowly . . .

Until finally the patient no longer experiences any discomfort being around a moose.

Unfortunately, some patients become so unafraid, a reverse situation develops and the patient begins to seek out that which once terrified him.

Frequently, this can lead to new phobia victims.

You now know enough about fear and phobias to be considered an expert. There remains, however, one unexplored area. An area so confusing, so bughouse, that few even dare bring it up. In Part III of this book, we shall detail some of the thousands of little-known

DEATH PHOBIAS

WHOOPSAPHOBIA

. . . fear of a small mud slide at your grave site.

B-B-QUEAPHOBIA

. . . fear of your cheap relatives trying to save money by having you cremated on a hibachi.

SLANTAPHOBIA

. . . fear of one of your pallbearers being a dwarf.

COLDCUTSAPHOBIA

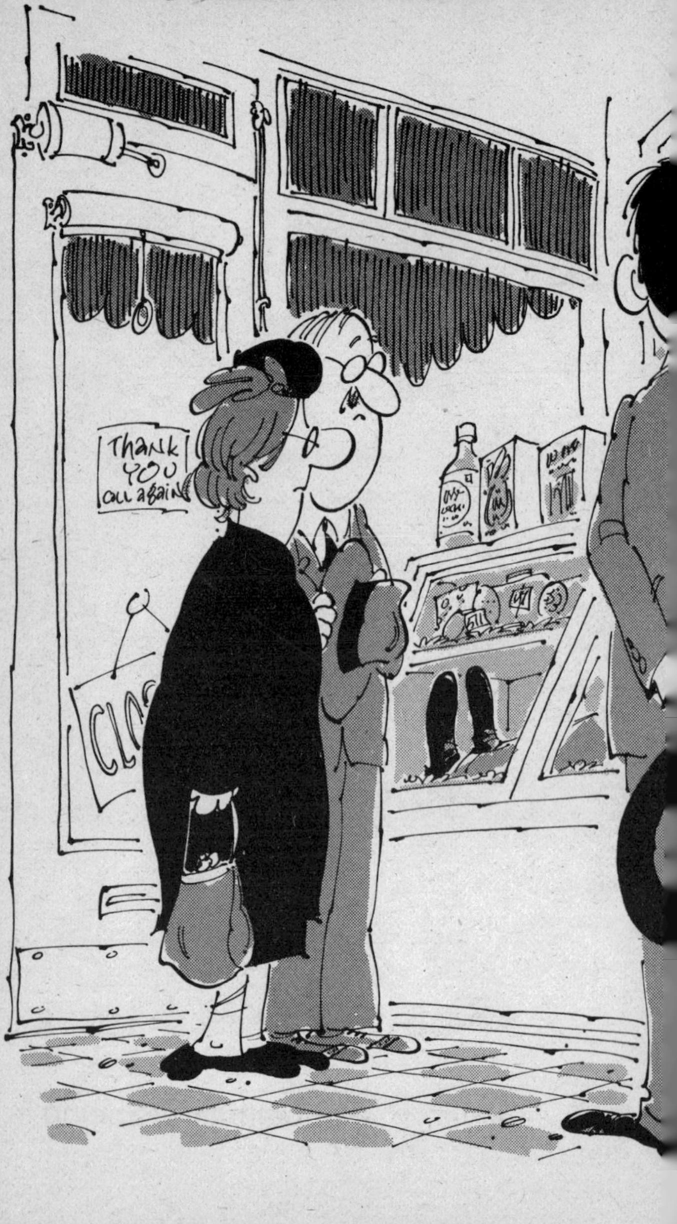

. . . fear of having your wake in a delicatessen.

THWIZZAPHOBIA

. . . fear of having your autopsy on New Year's Eve.

SANDBARAPHOBIA

. . . fear of being buried at sea during low tide.

LAPSEDAPHOBIA

. . . fear of your life insurance policy
expiring two weeks before you do.

SOFTSHOEAPHOBIA

. . . fear of someone tap dancing at your wake.

PEANUTBUTTERAPHOBIA

. . . fear of sticking to the
roof of your coffin.

Medical Phobias

DADAPHOBIA

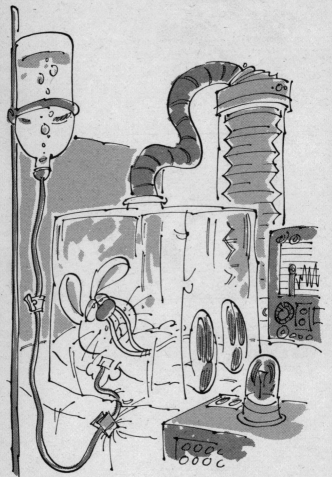

. . . fear of the rabbit in your girlfriend's pregnancy test being kept alive by artificial means.

NICKEDAPHOBIA

. . . fear of your doctor developing hiccups during your hernia operation.

MOLARAPHOBIA

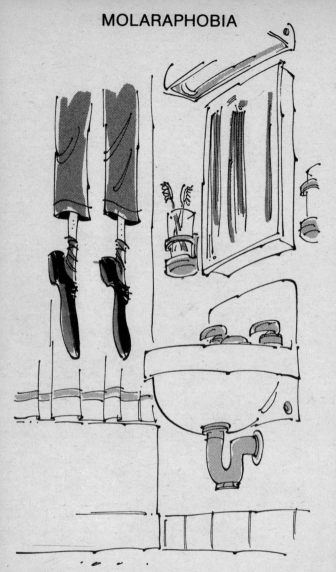

. . . fear of accidentally hanging yourself while flossing.

DIVORCEEAPHOBIA

. . . fear of giving your mother a kiss goodby and catching herpes.

SUBSCRIBEAPHOBIA

. . . fear of being buried alive under an
avalanche of lap cards.

SPORTS PHOBIAS

His palms are sweaty! His knees are knocking! If this isn't the agony of phobia, then I don't know what is!

ON-DECKAPHOBIA

. . . fear of coming home and finding your wife swinging with a designated hitter.

SPITAPHOBIA

. . . fear of slipping and drowning in the tobacco juice on the floor of a baseball dugout.

PASSAPHOBIA

. . . fear of a tight-end patting you on your behind whether you make a good play or not.

BUNTAPHOBIA

. . . fear of a sex-crazed third base coach
flashing signs to your wife.

... fear of a gastrointestinal explosion in the huddle.

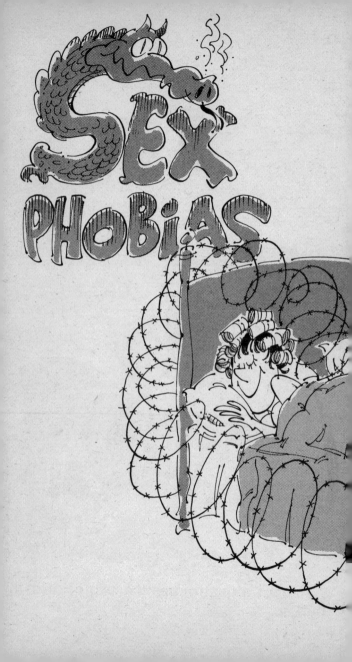

VISAPHOBIA

... fear of discovering the blind date you were fixed up with accepts all major credit cards.

NUKEDAPHOBIA

. . . fear of finding out on your wedding night that your best man had already launched a "preemptive first strike" on your new bride.

TRAMPAPHOBIA

. . . fear of discovering a speed bump in your girlfriend's bedroom doorway.

OPECAPHOBIA

. . . fear of running out of gas while dating
a girl much younger than you.

SiLLY
PHOBiAS

GNIP ... POP ... YEOWAPHOBIA

... fear of a crazed toll collector grabbing
your arm as you drive through.

ZAPAPHOBIA

. . . fear of having a bed-wetting accident while using your electric blanket.

CHOPPERAPHOBIA

. . . fear of your waitress dropping her teeth in your dinner plate.

SLOBBERAPHOBIA

. . . fear of baby drool.

DAMPAPHOBIA

. . . fear of discovering you put your boxer shorts on backwards — after drinking a six pack of beer.

CLUCKEDAPHOBIA

. . . fear of being permanently injured by a
flying chicken bone dislodged during the
Heimlich Maneuver.

Phobias for our MAD Society

WA
TCH YO
UR ST
EP

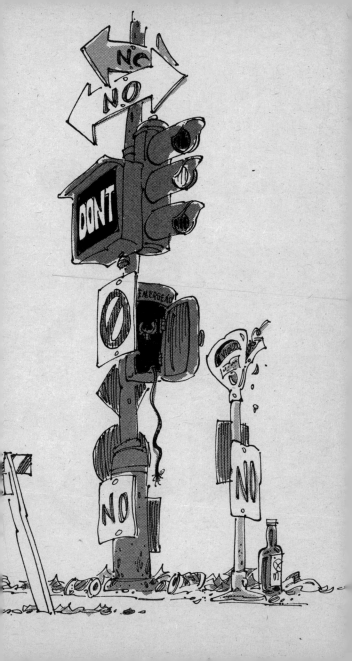

THUGSAPHOBIA

. . . fear of overhearing two muggers
arguing over who saw you first.

THERE-GOES-THE-PROM-APHOBIA

. . . fear of your school's new principal's first name being "Ayatollah."

TRANSAPHOBIA

. . . fear of finding out that the only thing you have in common with the girl you just picked up is that you're both boys.

SCRAPEAPHOBIA

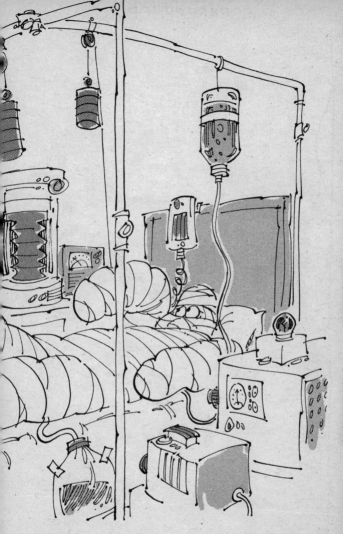

. . . fear of being struck by a tragedy big enough to wreck your life but not special enough to be parlayed into a TV Movie-Of-The-Week deal.

. . . fear of department stores pushing up the date they start decorating for Christmas to March 17.

AWARDSAPHOBIA

. . . fear of a TV network developing a new awards show to award awards for the best award shows of the previous year, including its own awards show .

AX-MURDERAPHOBIA

. . . fear of the homicidal maniac you
testified against being released on a
technicality.

GHETTOPHOBIA

... fear of some local preservation group having your slum declared an "historical landmark" just as urban renewal funds become available.

CORPAPHOBIA